Nanine
Voltaire
Translation by William F. Fleming

Start Publishing PD LLC
Copyright © 2024 by Start Publishing PD LLC

All rights reserved, including the right to reproduce this book or portions thereof in any form whatsoever.

Start Publishing PD is a registered trademark of Start Publishing PD LLC
Manufactured in the United States of America

Cover art: Shutterstock/Taisiya Kozorez

Cover design: Jennifer Do

10 9 8 7 6 5 4 3 2 1

ISBN 979-8-8809-0868-4

Contents

Dramatis Personæ. 4
Act I. 5
Act II. 21
Act III. 37

Dramatis Personæ

The Count d'Olban, a nobleman retired into the country.
The Baroness de l'Orme, a relation of the Count's, a haughty, imperious woman, of a bad temper, and disagreeable to live with.
The Marchioness d'Olban, mother of the Count.
Nanine, a young girl, brought up in the Count's house.
Philip Hombert, a peasant in the neighborhood.
Blaise, the gardener.
Germon, servant.
Marin, servant.

Scene, the Count d'Olban's country seat.

This Comedy is called in the French Nanine, ou le Préjugé Vaincu (Nanine, or Prejudice Overcome). It is written, as we are told in the title-page, in verses of ten syllables. The absurdity of comedies in rhyme I have already remarked. The original begins thus:

Il faut parler, il faut, Monsieur le Comte,
Vous expliquer nettement sur mon Compte.

The reader cannot but observe, what villainous rhymes Comte and Compte are, and perhaps will more readily forgive my reducing this comedy into plain prose. It was produced in 1749.

ACT I.

SCENE I.

The Count D'Olban, the Baroness De L'Orme.

Baroness: In short, my lord, it is time to come to an explanation with regard to this affair; we are no children; therefore, let us talk freely: you have been a widower for these two years past, and I, a widow about as long: the lawsuit in which we were unfortunately engaged, and which gave us both so much uneasiness, is at an end; and all our animosities, I hope, now buried with those who were the causes of them.

Count: I am glad of it; for lawsuits were always my aversion.

Baroness: And am not I as hateful as a lawsuit?

Count: You, madam?

Baroness: Yes, I, sir: for these two years past we have lived together, with freedom, as relations and friends; the ties of blood, taste, and interest, seem to unite us, and to point out a more intimate connection.

Count: Interest, madam? make use of some better term, I beseech you.

Baroness: That, sir, I cannot; but with grief I find, your inconstant heart no longer considers me in any other light than as your relative.

Count: I do not wear the appearance, madam, of a trifler.

Baroness: You wear the appearance, sir, of a perjured villain.

Count: [Aside.] Ha! what's this?

Baroness: Yes, sir: you know the suit my husband began against you, to recover my estate, was, by agreement, to have been terminated by a marriage; a marriage you told me, of choice; you are engaged to me, you know you are; and he who defers the execution of his promise seldom means to perform it.

Count: You know, I wait for my mother's consent.

Baroness: A doting old woman: well, sir, and what then?

Count: I love and respect her yet.

Baroness: But I do not, sir. Come, come, these are idle, frivolous excuses for your unpardonable falsehood: you wait not for her, or for anybody; perfidious, ungrateful man!

Count: Who told you so, madam, and whence all this violence of passion? who told you so? whence comes your information, madam?

Baroness: Who told me? yourself, yourself. Your words, your manner, your air, your whole behavior, put on on purpose to affront me: it shocks me to see it: act in another manner, or find some better excuses for your conduct: can you think me blind to the shameful, unworthy passion that directs you, a passion for the lowest, meanest object? you have deceived me, sir, basely deceived me.

Count: 'Tis false, I cannot deceive; dissimulation is no part of my character. I own to you, there was a time when you were agreeable to me; I admired you, and flattered myself that I should have found in you a treasure to make amends for that which heaven had deprived me of; I hoped in this sweet asylum to have tasted the fruits of a peaceful and happy union: but you have found out the means to destroy your own power. Love, as I told you long since, has two quivers: one filled with darts, tipped with the purest flame, which inspires the soul with tender feelings, refines our taste and sentiments, enlivens our affection, and enhances our pleasures; the other is full of cruel arrows, that wound our hearts with quarrels, jealousy, and suspicion, bring on coldness and indifference, and remove the warmth of passion to make room for disgust and satiety: these, madam, are the darts which you have drawn forth, against us both, and yet you expect that I should love.

Baroness: There, indeed, I own myself in the wrong: I ought not to expect it: it is not in your power: but you are false, and now would reproach me for it, and I must suffer your insults, your fine similes and illustrations: but pray, sir, what is it I have done to lose this mighty treasure? what have you to find fault with?

Count: Your temper, your humors, madam: beauty pleases the eye alone, softness and complacency charm the soul.

Baroness: And have not you your humors, too, sir?

Count: Doubtless, madam; and, for that very reason, would have an indulgent wife; one whose sweet complying goodness would bend a little to my frailties, and condescend to reconcile me to myself, to heal my wounds without burning them, to correct without assuming, to govern without being a tyrant, to insinuate herself by degrees into my heart, as the light of a fine day opens gradually on the weak and delicate eye: he who feels the yoke that is put on him will always murmur at it; and tyrannic love is a deity that I abjure: I would be a lover, but not a slave: your pride, madam, would make me contemptible: I have faults, I own I have; but heaven made woman to correct the leaven of our souls, to soften our afflictions, sweeten our bad humors, soothe our passions, and make us better and happier beings: this was what they were designed for; and, for my part, I would prefer ugliness and affability to beauty with pride and arrogance.

Baroness: Excellently well moralized, indeed; and so when you insult, abuse, and betray me, I in return, with mean complacency, must forgive the shameful extravagance of your passion; and your assumed air of grandeur and magnanimity must be a sufficient excuse to me for all the baseness of your heart.

Count: How, madam?

Baroness: Yes, sir: I know you: it is the young Nanine who has done me this injury; a child, a servant, a field beggar, whom my foolish tenderness nourished and supported; whom your fond, easy mother, touched with false pity, took up out of the bosom of penury and sorrow. O you blush, sir, do you?

Count: I, madam? I wish her well.

Baroness: You love her, sir: I know you do.

Count: Well, madam, and if I did love her, know, I would openly avow it.

Baroness: Nay, I believe you are capable of it.

Count: I am so.

Baroness: And would you break thus through all the bounds of decency, degrade your rank, demean your birth, and, plunged as you are in shame and infamy, laugh at and defy all honor?

Count: Call it prejudice: whatever you, or the world may think, madam, I never mistake vanity for honor and glory: you love pomp and splendor, and place grandeur and nobility in a coat of arms: I look for it in the heart. The man of worth, who has modesty with courage, and the woman who has sense and spirit, though without fortune, rank, or title, are, in my eyes, the first of human kind.

Baroness: But surely they ought to have some rank and condition in life. Would you treat a low-born scholar, or an honest man of the meanest birth, because he had a little virtue, in the same manner and with the same respect as you would a lord?

Count: The virtuous should always have the preference.

Baroness: This extravagant humility is insupportable: do we owe nothing then to our rank?

Count: Yes: to be honest.

Baroness: My noble blood would aspire to a higher character.

Count: That is a high one which defies the vulgar.

Baroness: Thus you degrade all quality.

Count: No: thus I do honor to humanity.

Baroness: Ridiculous! what then becomes of the world? what is fashion?

Count: Fashion, madam, is despised by wisdom: I will obey its ridiculous commands in my dress perhaps, but not in my sentiments: no: it becomes a man to act like a man, to preserve to himself his own taste and his own thoughts: am

I ridiculously to ask of others what I am to seek, or to avoid, to praise, or condemn? must the world decide my fate? surely I have my reason, and that should be my guide: apes were made for imitation only, but man should act from his own heart.

Baroness: Why, this, to be sure, is freedom of sentiment, and talking like a philosopher. Go, then, thou noble and sublime soul, go, and fall in love with village damsels, be the happy rival of plowmen and hedgers: go, and support the honor of your race.

Count: Good heaven! what must I do? How am I to act?

SCENE II.

The Count, the Baroness, Blaise.

Count: Well, sir, what do you want?

Blaise: Your poor gardener, sir, humbly beseeches your honor—

Count: My honor! well, Blaise, and what wouldst thou have of my honor?

Blaise: And please, your honor, I would fain—be married and—

Count: With all my heart, Blaise, you have my consent; I like your design, and will assist you. It is well folks should marry. Well, and thy spouse elect, Blaise, what is she? handsome?

Blaise: O yes, sir, a delicate little morsel.

Baroness: And does she like you, Blaise?

Blaise: O yes.

Count: Well, and her name is?

Blaise: Yes, 'tis—

Count: What?

Blaise: The pretty Nanine.

Count: Nanine?

Baroness: Well, very well indeed! I approve of the match extremely.

Count: [Aside.] O heaven! how am I sunk! it cannot, must not be.

Blaise: I'm sure, master will like it.

Count: What! did you say she loved you, rascal?

Blaise: I beg pardon, sir, I—

Count: Did she tell you that she loved you, sir?

Blaise: Why, no, sir, not absolutely, sir; not directly; but she seemed to have a little sort of a sneaking kindness for me, too: a hundred times has she said to me in the prettiest, softest, most familiar tone, "Help me, my dear friend Blaise, to make a fine nosegay for my lord, that best of masters;" then would she make the nosegay with such a pretty air, and look so thoughtful, and so absent, and so confused, and so—O it was plain enough.

Count: [Aside.] Away, Blaise, get thee gone—Oh! and am I agreeable to her then?

Blaise: Nay, master, now don't put off this little affair of mine.

Count: Ha!

Blaise: You shall see how this little spot of land will thrive under our hands soon: why won't you answer me, sir? You say nothing.

Count: [Aside.] Oh! my heart is too full: I must retire—madam, your servant.

SCENE III.

The Baroness, Blaise.

Baroness: [To herself.] He loves her to distraction, of that I'm positive: by what charms, by what happy address, could she thus steal his heart from me? Nanine! good heaven! what a choice! what madness! Nanine! no! I shall burst with disappointment.

Blaise: What did you say, madam, about Nanine?

Baroness: [To herself.] Insolent creature!

Blaise: Is not Nanine a charming girl?

Baroness: No.

Blaise: Well, I say no more; but do speak for me, speak for poor Blaise.

Baroness: What a dreadful stroke is this!

Blaise: I have a little money, madam, a few crowns: my father left me three good acres of land, and they shall be hers; money, and land, everything I have, body and soul, Blaise and all.

Baroness: Believe me, Blaise, I wish you as well as you can wish yourself, and should be glad to serve you: I should be glad to see you married this very night: nay, what's more, I'll give her a portion.

Blaise: O good, dear baroness! how I do love you! is it possible you can make me so happy?

Baroness: Alas! Blaise, I am afraid I cannot; we shall never succeed.

Blaise: O but you must, madam.

Baroness: I wish to God she was your wife: wait for my orders.

Blaise: And must I wait? not long I hope.

Baroness: Be gone.

Blaise: Servant, madam: I shall have hear, I shall have her.

SCENE IV.

Baroness: [Alone.] What a strange adventure! could I have received a more cruel injury? a more shameful affront? the Count d'Olban rivalled by a gardener—here, boy, [she calls out to her servant] fetch Nanine to me: since I am so unhappy, I must examine her: where could she have learned this art of flattery? who taught her to gain hearts, and to preserve them, to light up a strong and a lasting flame? where? doubtless, in her eyes, in plain and simple nature: but this shameful and unworthy passion of his is still a secret; it has not dared as yet to appear openly. D'Olban, I see, has his scruples about it: so much the worse; if he had none, I might still have hopes; but he has all the symptoms of true love: O here she comes, the sight of her hurts me; nature is most unjust, to bestow so much beauty on such a creature; 'tis an affront to nobility: come this way, madam.

SCENE V.

The Baroness, Nanine.

Nanine: Madam.

Baroness: And yet, after all, she is not so very handsome; those great black eyes of hers express nothing; but if they have said, I love; ay, there's the danger: but I must—come this way, child.

Nanine: I come, madam, as is my duty.

Baroness: Yes: but you make me wait a little for you; prithee, child, step on: how awkwardly she is made! what a mien there is! he was never made for such a creature as you.

Nanine: 'Tis very true, madam: I assure you; I have often blushed in secret when I looked on these fine clothes: but they were your first present to me, the effect of that goodness which I shall ever acknowledge, and of that generous care with which you were pleased to honor me: you took a pride in dressing me: O madam, remember how often you have protected me: believe me, madam, I am still the same: why should you wish to humble a submissive heart, which can never forget itself?

Baroness: Bring that couch nearer to me—O I am distracted: whence come you? what have you been about?

Nanine: Reading, madam.

Baroness: Reading what?

Nanine: An English book that was given me.

Baroness: What's the subject of it?

Nanine: 'Tis extremely interesting: the author would have us believe that we are all brethren, all born equal, and on a level with each other; but 'tis an idle chimera, I can't reconcile myself to his doctrine.

Baroness: [Aside.] She will soon, I suppose—what vanity! [To Nanine] bring me my standish, and pen and ink.

Nanine: Yes, madam.

Baroness: No; stay: give me something to drink.

Nanine: What, madam?

Baroness: Nothing: it's no matter: take my fan. Go and get my gloves—or—stay—it does not signify, you need not: come hither: I desire you to take care never to think yourself handsome.

Nanine: That, madam, is a lesson you have so often taught me that if I had so much vanity, and self-love had such influence over my foolish heart, you would soon have cured me of it.

Baroness: [Aside.] Where can she have learned all this? how I hate her! beauty and wit together! 'tis intolerable—hark'ee, child, you know the tenderness I had for you in your infancy.

Nanine: Yes, madam, and I hope my youth will be honored with equal goodness from you.

Baroness: Be careful then to deserve it: it is my intention now, this very day, nay, this very hour, to fix and establish your happiness; judge then whether I love you.

Nanine: To fix my happiness?

Baroness: Yes: I will give you a portion: the husband I design for you is well-made, and in every way worthy of you; a proper match for you in every particular, and the only one that at present could suit you: you ought to thank me for the choice: in a word, 'tis Blaise, the gardener.

Nanine: Blaise, madam?

Baroness: Yes: why that simpering? do you hesitate a moment to consent? my offers, madam, I would have you know, are commands; obey, or expect my resentment.

Nanine: But, madam—

Baroness: Let me have no buts; they offend me: a pretty thing indeed, for your impertinence to refuse a husband at my hands! that simple heart of yours is swelled to a fine degree of vanity: but your boldness is a little premature, and your triumph will be of short duration: you take advantage of the capricious fortune of one lucky day, but shall soon see what will be the event. You ungrateful little wretch, have you the insolence to please? you understand me, madam, but I'll bring you back to that nothingness whence you came, and you shall lament your folly and your pride: I'll shut you up for the rest of your life in a convent.

Nanine: On my knees I thank you, madam; do shut me up, my fate will be too mild: yes, madam, of all the benefits you have ever bestowed on me, this, which you call a punishment, I shall esteem the greatest favor: shut me up forever in a cloister; there, I will thank you for your goodness, and bless my dear master: there I shall learn to calm those cruel fears, those dreadful alarms, those worst of evils, those passions that are far more dangerous to me even than your resentment, which fill me with terror and astonishment: O madam, by that anger, I entreat you, deliver me, save me, save me, if possible, from myself; this moment I am ready to go.

Baroness: What do I hear? can it be? are you in earnest, Nanine, or mean you to deceive me?

Nanine: No: indeed I do not. O do me this charming, this divine favor; my heart stands too much in need of it.

Baroness: [With transport.] Rise then, and let me embrace you. O happy hour! my dear Nanine, my friend, I'll go this instant and prepare your sweet retreat; O 'tis a charming thing to live in a convent!

Nanine: 'Tis at least a shelter from the world, and all its cares.

Baroness: O my dear, 'tis a delightful situation.

Nanine: Do you think so, madam?

Baroness: This world is a hateful place—jealous—

Nanine: [Sighing.] 'Tis so indeed.

Baroness: Foolish, wicked, vain, deceitful, inconstant, and ungrateful: O 'tis a horrid place.

Nanine: Yes, I see it would be fatal to me, I ought to flee from it.

Baroness: You ought indeed: a good convent is the best haven of security. Now, my good lord, I think I shall be beforehand with you.

Nanine: Did you say anything about my master, madam?

Baroness: O Nanine, I love you even to madness: this moment I would, if possible, lock you up never to come out again: but to-night it is too late, we must wait till morning. Hark'ee, child, come to me at midnight to my apartment, and we will set off secretly for the convent: be ready by five at the latest.

SCENE VI.

Nanine: [Alone.] How distressful is my condition! what trouble and uneasiness do I feel! and what various passions rise in my soul! to leave so good, so amiable a master, perhaps to offend him by it: and yet, if I had stayed, this excess of his goodness might have brought on worse calamities, and put his whole family in confusion. The baroness seems apprehensive that he has a particular regard for me: but his heart could never stoop so low; I must not, dare not think of it: and my lady seems desperately angry about it: am I hated then, and should I be afraid of being beloved? O but myself, myself I have most reason to fear, and my foolish heart, that beats so at the thought of him. What will become of me? taken out of my humble state, my notions now are too refined and too exalted: it is a misfortune, nay, and it is a fault, too, to have a mind above one's condition. I must go: I know it will kill me: but no matter.

SCENE VII.

The Count, Nanine, a Servant.

Count: Stay at that door there somebody, d'ye hear? bring chairs here, quick, make haste. [He bows to Nanine, who makes him a low courtesy.] Come, sit down.

Nanine: Who, I, sir?

Count: Yes: I will have it so: I mean to pay you, Nanine, that respect which your conduct, your beauty, and merit deserve: shines the diamond with less lustre, or is it less valuable, because found in a desert? What's the matter? your eyes seem bathed in tears: O I see it but too plainly; our angry baroness, jealous of your charms, has been venting her ill-humors on you, and left my poor girl weeping.

Nanine: No, sir, no: her goodness, I assure you, to me was never greater than at present; but everything here softens and affects me.

Count: I'm glad to hear it; I was afraid it was some of her malice.

Nanine: Why so, sir?

Count: O my dear girl, jealousy reigns in every breast: every man is jealous when he is in love, and every woman even before she is so. A young and beautiful girl, who at the same time is good-natured and sincere, is sure to displease her whole sex: men are more just, and we endeavor as well as we can to revenge ourselves on you for your jealousy: but, with regard to Nanine, I only do her justice, I love that heart which is void of artifice; I admire the display of those extraordinary talents which you have so finely cultivated; and I am both surprised and charmed at the ingenuous simplicity of your manners.

Nanine: O sir, my merit is small indeed; but I have seen you, have heard and been instructed by you: you have raised me too high above my humble birth: I owe you but too much: from you only I have learned to think.

Count: O Nanine, wit and good sense are not to be taught.

Nanine: I think too much, I fear, for one in my station: my fortune designed me for the lowest rank in life.

Count: Your virtues have placed you in the highest: but tell me ingenuously, what effect had that English book I lent you?

Nanine: Not convinced me at all, sir: I am more than ever of opinion, that there are hearts so noble and so generous, that all others must appear mean and vile when put in comparison with them.

Count: True, Nanine, and you are yourself a proof of it: but permit me to raise you for the future to a rank and station here less unworthy of you.

Nanine: My condition, sir, is already too high, and too desirable for me.

Count: No, Nanine, that cannot be: henceforward I shall consider you as one of the family; my mother is coming, she will look on you as her daughter, my esteem, and her tender friendship, will put you on a different footing, and place you in a better rank than you have hitherto held under a proud and imperious woman.

Nanine: [Aside.] She only taught me my duty, sir—and a hard one it is to fulfil.

Count: What duty? yours, Nanine, is only to please, and that you always perform; would I could do so, too! but you should be more at your ease, and appear with more splendor; you are not yet in your proper sphere.

Nanine: I am indeed quite out of it, and it is that which makes me unhappy; 'tis my misfortune, perhaps an irreparable one. [Rising.] O my lord, my master, remove, I beseech you, from me all these vanities: I am confused, overwhelmed with your excess of goodness; let me live unknown and unenvied; heaven formed me for obscurity, and humility has nothing in it that to me is grating or disagreeable: leave me to my retreat; what should I do in the world, what should I wish to see there, after the admiration of your virtues?

Count: [To himself.] It is too much, I can resist no longer. [To Nanine.] You remain in obscurity? you?

Nanine: Whatever I may do, permit me to ask one favor of you.

Count: What is it? speak.

Nanine: For some time past you have loaded me with presents.

Count: Pardon me, Nanine, I acted but as a tender father who loved his child: I have not the art to set off my presents by flattery, I aim not at gallantry, and only desire to be just: fortune had done you wrong, and I meant to avenge the injury: but nature, in recompense for it, lavished all her bounties on you, and her I strove to imitate.

Nanine: You have done a great deal too much; but I flatter myself I may be permitted, without being thought ungrateful, to dispose of those noble presents, which I shall ever hold dear because they came from you.

Count: You mean to affront me, sure.

SCENE VIII.

The Count, Nanine, Germon.

Germon: My lady wants you; she waits.

Count: Let her wait then: what! can't I speak a moment to you without being interrupted?

Nanine: It gives me pain to leave you; but you know, sir, she was my mistress.

Count: No: I know it not, nor ever will.

Nanine: She has still a power over me.

Count: No such thing: she shall have none—you sigh, Nanine, there's something at the bottom of that heart; what's the matter?

Nanine: I am sorry to leave you, sir—but I must—O heaven, now all is over. [She goes out.]

SCENE IX.

The Count, Germon.

Count: [To himself.] She wept as she left me; for a long time she has groaned beneath the tyrannical caprice of this peevish baroness, who insults her: and by what right, or what authority? but 'tis an abuse which I will never suffer: this world is nothing but a lottery of wealth, titles, dignities, rights, and privileges, bartered for without legal claim, and scattered without distinction—here, you—

Germon: My lord.

Count: To-morrow morning lay this purse of a hundred louis d'ors on her toilette; be sure you don't fail; you must then go and see after her servants below, they'll wait there.

Germon: The baroness shall certainly have them on her toilette according to your orders.

Count: Blockhead, they're not for her: for Nanine, I tell you.

Germon: O very well, sir, I beg pardon.

Count: Begone, leave me. [Germon goes out.] This tenderness of mine can never be a weakness in me: true, I idolize her; but my heart was not touched by her beauty only, her character is to the last degree amiable: I admire her soul; but then her low condition—it is too high; were she lower, I should love her yet more: but can I marry her? doubtless I may; can one pay too dear for being happy? shall I fear the censure of an idle world, and let pride deprive me of all I wish for? but then custom—a cruel tyrant: nature has a prior right, and should be obeyed: and so I am Blaise's rival, too; and why not? Blaise is a man; he loves her, and he is in the right of it: she can be but in the possession of one, though the desire of all: gardeners may sigh for her, and so may kings: my happiness will justify my choice.

ACT II.

SCENE I.

The Count, Marin.

Count: [To himself.] Well; this night is a whole year to me: not once have I closed my eyelids: everybody is asleep but me; Nanine sleeps in peace, a sweet repose refreshes her charms, while I wander from place to place, and can find no rest: I sit down to write, but can't: then strive to read, but all in vain; I don't know the words before me while I am looking on them, nor can my mind retain a single idea: methinks, in every page, I see the name of Nanine imprinted by some hand divine—hullo! who's there? all asleep? German, Marin.

Marin: [Behind the scenes.] Coming, sir.

Count: You idle rascals, make haste, it's broad daylight; come, come.

Marin: Lord, sir, what spirit has raised you up so early this morning?

Count: Love.

Marin: O ho! my lady will let none of us sleep long in this house; what did you want, sir?

Count: Why, Marin, I must have, let me see, by to-morrow at the latest, six new horses, a new equipage, a clever chambermaid, notable and careful, a valet de chambre, and two footmen, young and well-made, and no libertines; some diamonds, some very fine buckles, some gold trinkets, and some new stuffs; therefore, be gone, ride post to Paris this instant, never mind killing a few horses.

Marin: O ho, I see how it is; you are caught; my lady baroness is to be our mistress to-day, I suppose; you are going to be married to her at last?

Count: Whatever my intention is, go you about your business; fly, and make haste back.

Marin: I'm gone, sir.
SCENE II.

The Count, Germon.

Count: [To himself.] And shall I then enjoy the sweet pleasure of honoring, of making happy the dear object of my love? The baroness, I know, will be in a rage: with all my heart, let her rave as long as she will; I despise her, and the world, and its opinion; and am afraid of nobody: I will never be the slave of prejudice; it is an enemy whom we ought to subdue, those who make a rational mind more virtuous, and those only are respectable: but hark! what noise is that in the court? a chariot sure: it must be so; yet who could come at this time in the morning? my mother perhaps. Germon—

Germon: Sir.

Count: What is that?

Germon: A chariot, sir.

Count: Whose is it? anybody coming here?

Germon: No, sir, they're going.

Count: Going? who? where?

Germon: The baroness, sir, going out immediately.

Count: O with all my heart, let her go forever if she pleases!

Germon: Nanine and she are this minute setting out.

Count: O heaven! what sayest thou? Nanine?

Germon: So the maid says, sir.

Count: How is this?

Germon: My lady, sir, is going with her this morning, to put her into a neighboring convent.

Count: Away: fly: let us begone: but what am I about? I am too warm to talk to them: no matter, I'll go; I ought—but stop, that must not be, I should at once discover all my passion: no—go, Germon, stop them, let everything be fast; bring Nanine to me, or answer it with your life. [Germon goes out.] So they would have carried her off! what a dreadful stroke! ungrateful, cruel, unjust woman! how have I deserved this! what have I done! I only loved and adored her; but never declared my passion; never endeavored to force her inclinations, or to alarm her timid innocence: why should she fly from me? the more I think of it, the more I am astonished.

SCENE III.

The Count, Nanine.

Count: My sweet girl, is it you? what, run away from me? answer me, explain this mystery to me: terrified, I suppose, with the baroness's threats, you were willing to escape; and that tender regard which I have long had for your virtues, I know, has quickened her resentment; surely you could not yourself have thought of leaving me, of depriving this place of its fairest ornament: last night, when I saw you in tears, tell me, Nanine, had you any intention of this? answer me, tell me, why would you have wished to leave me?

Nanine: Behold me on my knees, and trembling before you.

Count: [Raising her up.] Rise, Nanine, and tell me—I tremble more myself.

Nanine: My lady, sir—

Count: Well—what of her?

Nanine: That lady, sir, whom I honor and esteem, did not, I assure you, force me to the convent.

Count: And could it then be your own choice? O misery!

Nanine: It was, I own it was: I entreated her to restrain my wandering thoughts—she wanted to marry me.

Count: Indeed? to whom?

Nanine: To your gardener.

Count: O the worthy choice!

Nanine: I, sir, was ashamed, and to the last degree unhappy: I who in vain endeavor to stifle sentiments far above my condition, I whom your bounty had raised too high, must now be punished by the loss of that goodness which I never deserved.

Count: You punish yourself, Nanine, and for what?

Nanine: For having dared to raise the resentment of your relation, sir, who was once my mistress; I know, sir, I am disagreeable to her; the very sight of me disgusts her: she has reason indeed, for when I was near her, I was guilty of a weakness which I shall ever feel; it grows on me every hour: but I would have torn it from my breast; I would have humbled, by the austerities of a convent, this proud heart, exalted by your goodness, and revenged on it the involuntary crime: but the bitterest grief I felt, was my fear of offending you.

Count: [Turning from her, and walking about.] What sentiments! what a noble and ingenuous mind! Can she be prejudiced in my favor? was she afraid of loving me? O exalted virtue!

Nanine: If I have offended you, I beg a thousand pardons; but permit me, sir, in some deep retreat to hide my sorrows, and to reflect in secret on my own duty, and your goodness to me.

Count: No more of that: now, observe me, the baroness is your friend, and out of her generosity has provided you with a servant, a rustic, a boor, for your husband. I know of one who will at least be less unworthy of you: in birth and fortune far superior to Blaise; young, honest, and well provided for: a man, I assure you, of sense and reflection: his character very different from those of the present age: if I am not much mistaken, he'll make you an excellent husband: is not this better than a convent?

Nanine: No: sir, I own to you, this new favor which you would bestow on me has nothing in it that can give me any real satisfaction: you know my grateful heart, read there my real sentiments, and see why I wish to retreat from the world: a gardener, or the monarch of the whole world, who should offer marriage to me, would be equally displeasing.

Count: You have determined me: and now, Nanine, know the man for whom I have designed you: you already esteem him: he is yours; he adores you: that husband is—myself. I see, you are troubled and surprised: but speak to me; my life depends on you: O recollect yourself, you are strangely agitated.

Nanine: What do I hear? can it be?

Count: It is no more than you deserve.

Nanine: In love with me? O do not think, do not imagine I will ever dare to claim my conquest: no, sir, never will I suffer you to descend thus low for me: such marriages, believe me, sir, are always unhappy: fancy vanishes, and repentance alone remains. No, I will call your ancestors to witness—alas! sir, think not on me: you took pity on my youth: this heart, which you have formed, which is your own work, would be unworthy of your care, if it could accept from you this noblest present. No, sir, I owe you at least this refusal: my heart shall sacrifice itself for your sake.

Count: No more: for I am resolved, and you shall be my wife. Did you not this moment assure me you would refuse every other man, though he were a prince?

Nanine: I did, and repent not of the resolution.

Count: Do you hate me then?

Nanine: Should I have fled, should I have avoided, should I have feared, if I had hated you?

Count: It is enough, and I am fixed.

Nanine: What then have you determined on?

Count: Our marriage.

Nanine: Think, sir.

Count: I have thought of everything.

Nanine: And foreseen too?

Count: I have.

Nanine: If you love me, believe me, sir—

Count: I do believe—that I have resolved on the only means to make myself happy.

Nanine: But you forget—

Count: I have forgotten nothing: everything is ordered, and everything shall be ready.

Nanine: What! in spite of all I say, will your obstinate passion—

Count: Yes, in spite of you, my impatient love must urge the happy moment. I will quit you for a minute, that henceforth we may never part: adieu, my dear Nanine.

SCENE IV.

Nanine: [Alone.] Good heaven! do I dream? or am I indeed arrived at the summit of earthly happiness? 'tis not the honor, great as it is; 'tis not the splendor that dazzles me: no: I despise it all: but to wed the most generous of men, the dear object of all my timid wishes, him whom I was so much afraid of loving, him whom I adore, yet I love him too much to wish he should demean himself for my sake: but it is impossible to avoid it; I cannot now escape him:

what can I do? heaven, I trust, will direct me, and support my weakness, perhaps even—but I'll write to him—and yet how to begin, and what to say—what a surprise! I will write immediately before I enter into this solemn engagement.

SCENE V.

Nanine, Blaise.

Blaise: O there she is: well, my little maid, my lady has spoken to you in my favor, has she not? ha! she writes on, and takes no notice of me.

Nanine: [Writing on.] O Blaise, good morrow to you.

Blaise: Good morrow is but a cold compliment.

Nanine: [Writing.] Every word I write doubles my distress, and my whole letter is full of doubts and uneasiness.

Blaise: How she writes offhand! O she's a great genius; and a monstrous wit: I wish I was a wit too, then I'd tell her—

Nanine: Well, sir.

Blaise: Lackaday, she's so clever, I'm afraid to speak: I shall never be able to break my mind to her yet I was hot upon't, and came here o' purpose; that I did.

Nanine: Dear Blaise, you must do me a piece of service.

Blaise: Marry, two an' you will.

Nanine: I shall trust to your discretion, to your good heart, Blaise; nay, I do you but justice.

Blaise: O no ceremony; for look you, ma'am, Blaise is ready to serve you, and there's an end of it. Come, come, make no secret.

Nanine: You often go to the neighboring village, to Remival, the right hand side of the road.

Blaise: Yes, yes.

Nanine: Could you find one Philip Hombert for me there?

Blaise: Philip Hombert? I know nothing of him: what sort of a man is he?

Nanine: He came there, I believe, but yesterday evening; do you look him up, and give him immediately this money, and this letter.

Blaise: Oh, money is it?

Nanine: And at the same time deliver him this packet: go on horse-back that you may return the sooner: away, make haste, and be assured I'll remember you for it.

Blaise: I would go for you to the world's end—this Philip Hombert is a happy rogue: the purse is full: all ready rhino. What, is it a debt?

Nanine: Yes: and well proved; nothing can be more sacred, therefore take care of it: hark'ee, Blaise, Hombert may not be known in the village, perhaps he is not yet returned: if you can't give the letter into his own hands, bring it me back again: my dear friend, remember that.

Blaise: My dear friend!

Nanine: I shall depend on you.

Blaise: Her dear friend! O lud!

Nanine: I rely entirely upon you, and expect everything from your fidelity.

SCENE VI.

The Baroness, Blaise.

Blaise: What a message! and where the deuce could this money come from? it would have been of service to me in housekeeping: but she has a friendship for me, and that's better than money, so away we go. [As he is putting the money and letter into his pocket, he meets the baroness, and runs full against her.]

Baroness: How now, booby? a little more and you'd have broken my head.

Blaise: I beg your pardon, madam.

Baroness: Where are you going? have you heard anything of Nanine? what is she about? is the count in a violent passion? what have you got there, a letter?

Blaise: O that's a secret: poise on her!

Baroness: Let me look at it.

Blaise: Nanine will be angry.

Baroness: Nanine! could she write, and send it by you? give it me this minute, or I'll break off your match immediately; give it me, I say.

Blaise: [Laughing.] He! he!

Baroness: What do you laugh at?

Blaise: [Still laughing.] Ah! ah!

Baroness: I must know the contents of this;—[Breaks open the letter] if I am not mistaken, they concern me nearly.

Blaise: [Laughing.] Ah! ah! ah! how she is nicked now! she has got nothing there but a scrap of paper: but I shall keep the money, and carry it to Philip Hombert: yes, yes, must obey my mistress. Servant, ma'am.

SCENE VII.

The Baroness: [Alone.] Now let's see what we have got. [Reads.] "Both my joy and tenderness are unspeakable, as is my happiness also: what a moment was this for you to come in! when I cannot see or hear you, cannot throw myself into your arms: but, I conjure you, take these packets, and accept the contents of them. Know, I have been offered a most noble and truly enviable condition in life, such as I might well be dazzled with the prospect of: but there is nothing which I would not sacrifice to the only one on earth whom my heart ought to love." Very fine indeed! upon my word, Nanine, an excellent style: how prettily she writes! the innocent orphan: her passion speaks most eloquently: a rare billet this! O thou sly jade: thus you deceived poor Blaise, and thus deprived me of my lover: this going into a convent, I find, was all a feint, a pretence; and the count's money, it seems, is for Philip Hombert: thou little coquette! but I am glad of it: the count's perfidiousness to me deserved this return: I thought indeed Nanine's heart was as mean as her birth, and now I am satisfied of it.

SCENE VIII.

The Count, Baroness.

Baroness: But here comes the philosopher, the sentimental Count d'Olban, the wise lover, the man above prejudice: your servant, noble count, approach and laugh, my dear lover, at the most ridiculous circumstance: do you know Philip Hombert, of Remival? but, to be sure, you can't be a stranger to your—rival.

Count: What is all this, pray?

Baroness: This billet perhaps will inform you: this Hombert must be a handsome lad.

Count: You are too late, madam, now with your schemes; my resolution once made, I am not to be shaken: be satisfied, madam, with the shameful trick you wanted to play me this morning.

Baroness: You'll find this new one worse, I believe: there, read: [Gives him the letter] you'll like it vastly: you know the hand, and you know the virtue of the dear nymph that has subdued you: [While he is reading it he seems confounded, grows pale and angry] well, sir, what think you of the style?—he sees nothing, says nothing, hears nothing: poor man! but he deserves it.

Count: Did I read aright? it cannot be. I am astonished, thunder-struck; ungrateful sex! perfidious creature!

Baroness: [Aside.] I know his temper well; naturally violent, quick and resolute: he'll do something immediately.

SCENE IX.

The Count, Baroness, Germon.

Germon: Yonder comes Madam d'Olban: she's in the avenue already.

Baroness: Is the old woman returned?

Germon: Sir, sir, my lady, your mother, is coming.

Baroness: His anger has taken away his hearing: the letter operates finely.

Germon: [Bawling out to him.] Sir.

Count: Does she think—

Germon: [Aloud.] My lady, sir, your mother.

Count: What is Nanine doing at this instant?

Germon: Writing in her own apartment—but, sir—

Count: [With an air of coolness.] Go, seize her papers; bring me what she writes, and then let her be sent away.

Germon: Who, sir?

Count: Nanine.

Germon: I can never have the heart to do it, sir: O sir, if you knew how she charms us all, so noble, so good!

Count: Do it, sir, or see my face no more.

Germon: I obey, sir. [He goes out.]

SCENE X.

The Count, Baroness.

Baroness: Now, the day is ours: I give you joy, sir, of your return to reason: now, sir, is it not true as I told you, the low-bred always retain something of their former condition, and persons of family alone have hearts truly noble? Blood, sir, let me tell you, does everything, and meanness of birth will inspire Nanine with sentiments you never suspected her of.

Count: That I don't believe: but come, we'll talk no more about it, but endeavor to make amends for past errors: every man has his follies, at some part of his life; we all go wrong; and he is least to blame who repents the soonest.

Baroness: 'Tis well observed.

Count: Never mention her to me again: be silent on that head, I entreat you.

Baroness: Most willingly.

Count: I beg this subject of our dispute may be entirely forgotten.

Baroness: But will you remember then your former vows?

Count: Well, well, I understand you, I will.

Baroness: And quickly, too, or you will not repair the injury: our marriage so shamefully deferred is an affront—

Count: That shall be made amends for; but, madam, we must have—

Baroness: Have what? we must have a lawyer.

Count: You know, madam, that—I waited for my mother.

Baroness: And here she comes.

SCENE XI.

The Marchioness D'olban, the Count, Baroness.

Count: [To his mother.] Madam, I should have—[Aside] O Philip Hombert! [To his mother] but you have prevented me: my respect and tenderness—[Aside] with that air of innocence too! perfidious wretch!

Marchioness: Why, you rave, child; I heard indeed, as I passed through Paris, that your head was a little touched, and I find there was some truth in it; how long has this misfortune—

Count: Good heaven! how confused I am!

Marchioness: Does it seize you often?

Count: It never will again, madam.

Marchioness: I should be glad to speak with you alone. [Turns to the baroness and makes her a formal courtesy.] Good morrow, madam.

Baroness: [Aside.] The old fool! [Turning to the Marchioness] Madam, I leave you the pleasure of entertaining the count at your leisure, and retire. [She goes out.]

SCENE XII.

The Marchioness, the Count.

Marchioness: [Talking very fast, and in the manner of a little prattling old woman.] Well, sir, and so you intend to make the baroness my daughter-in-law: 'twas this, to tell you the truth, that brought me here so soon: she's a peevish, impertinent, proud, opinionated creature, and one who never had the least regard for me: last year, when I supped with the Marchioness Agard, she said before all the company, I was a babbler. Lord forbid I should ever sup there again: a babbler! besides, I know, between you and me, she is not so rich; and that, let me tell you, son, is a great point, and we ought to be well-informed about it: they tell me that the Château d'Orme did but half of it belong to her husband, and that the other half was disputed by a long lawsuit, that is not finished to this day: that I had from your grandpapa, and he always told the truth: ay, he was a man; there are few such nowadays: there is nothing now at Paris but a set of half-men, vain, foolish, impertinent coxcombs, talking on every subject, and laughing at times past. Oh, their eternal clack distracts me, prating about new kitchens, and new fashions: we hear of nothing now but bankrupts, and distress, and ruin: the wives, in short, are licentious, and the husbands simpletons: everything grows worse and worse.

Count: [Reading the letter over again.] Who could have thought it? this is a desperate stroke indeed. Well, Germon?

SCENE XIII.

The Marchioness, the Count, Germon.

Germon: Here's your lawyer, sir.

Count: O let him wait.

Germon: And here's the paper, sir, she sent you.

Count: [Reading.] Give it me—well, let me see: she loves me, she says here, and refuses me out of—respect. Faithless woman! thou hast not told me the true reason of that refusal.

Marchioness: My son's head is certainly turned: 'tis the baroness's doing: love has taken away his senses.

Count: [To Germon.] Is Nanine gone! shall I be rid of her?

Germon: Alas! sir, she has already put on her old rustic garb with the greatest modesty, and never murmured or complained.

Count: Very likely so.

Germon: She bore her misfortune with the utmost tranquillity, while everybody about her was in tears.

Count: With tranquillity, sayest thou?

Marchioness: Whom are you talking about?

Germon: O madam, poor Nanine, she is going to be driven away, and everybody laments the loss of her.

Marchioness: To be driven away? how is this? I don't understand it: what! my little Nanine go! call her back again: my charming orphan! what has she done, pray? why, Nanine was my present to you. O I remember, at ten years of age she delighted everybody that saw her: our baroness took her, and I said then she would be ill-used; I knew it would be so: but you never mind what I say; you will do everything of your own head: but let me tell you, turning Nanine out of doors thus is a very bad action.

Count: Alone, on foot, without money, without assistance!

Germon: O sir, I forgot to tell you: an old man asked after you below, and says he wants to speak to you on an affair of importance, which he can communicate to none but yourself: he wants to throw himself at your feet.

Count: In my present unhappy situation of mind, am I fit to converse with anybody?

Marchioness: You are uneasy enough, I believe, child, and so am I, too, to drive away poor Nanine, and make up a marriage which you knew would be disagreeable to me: come, it was not a wise thing: in three months' time you will be weary of one another: I'll tell you what happened exactly like this to my cousin the Marquis of Marmure: his wife was as sour as verjuice, though, by the by, yours is worse; when they married, they thought they loved one another, and in two months after they were parted. My lady went to live with her gallant, a foolish, sharking, extravagant fop; and my lord took a vile, tricking, ridiculous coquette! fine suppers, country houses, horses, clothes, a rascally steward, new trinkets bought on trust, lawyers, contracts, interest-money, all together soon ruined them, and in two years both went together to the hospital. O, and now

I think of it, I remember another story, more tragical, and more extraordinary than the other, it was of a—

Count: My dear mother, we must go in to dinner: come—could I ever have suspected such infidelity!

Marchioness: 'Tis really dreadful: but I'll tell it you all at table: in proper time and place, son, it may be of great use to you. Away.

ACT III.

SCENE I.

Nanine, Clothed as a Country Girl, Germon.

Germon: We are all in tears at the thought of losing you.

Nanine: It is time to go: I've staid too long already.

Germon: But you won't leave us forever, I hope, and in this dress, too?

Nanine: Obscurity was my first condition.

Germon: What a change! and only from this morning: to suffer is nothing, but to be degraded is terrible.

Nanine: No, no, there are a thousand times worse misfortunes.

Germon: I admire your patience and humility; surely my master must have been ill-advised: our baroness has certainly abused her power: she must have done you this injury, the count could never have the heart.

Nanine: I am indebted to him for everything; and, if he thinks fit to banish me, I must submit; his favors are his own, and he has a right to recall them.

Germon: Who would ever have expected such a change? what do you intend to do with yourself?

Nanine: To retire, and repent.

Germon: How we shall all detest the baroness!

Nanine: They have made me miserable, but I forgive them.

Germon: But what shall I tell my master from you when you are gone?

Nanine: Tell him, I thank him for restoring me to my former condition: tell him that, forever sensible of his goodness, I shall forget nothing but his—cruelty.

Germon: You melt my very soul; I could leave this house immediately to go along with you wherever you went: but Blaise is beforehand with us all: he will go and live with you, and we are all ready to follow him.

Nanine: No, Germon, that I'm sure you are not. O Germon, to be driven out in this manner—and by whom?

Germon: The devil is certainly at the bottom of this business: you are leaving us, and my master is going to be married.

Nanine: Married, sayest thou? indeed? nay, then let us be gone: O he was too dangerous for me—farewell.

Germon: Well! after all, my master must have a cruel heart, to banish so sweet a creature: she seems a most amiable girl, but in this world one should swear to nothing.

SCENE II.

The Count, Germon.

Count: Well, is she gone at last?

Germon: Yes, sir, 'tis done.

Count: I'm glad of it.

Germon: Then, sir, you have a heart of iron.

Count: Did Philip Hombert meet and give her his hand?

Germon: What Philip Hombert, sir? alas! sir, poor Nanine went off without a creature to give her his hand; she would not even accept of mine.

Count: And where is she gone?

Germon: That I know not; most probably to her friends.

Count: Ay, at Remival, I suppose.

Germon: Yes, I believe she went that road.

Count: Go, Germon, immediately, and conduct her to that convent where the baroness was going this morning, I'll lodge her in that safe retreat: these hundred louis d'ors will secure her reception; carry them to her, but take care she does not know they come from me: tell her 'tis a present from my mother: on no account mention my name to her.

Germon: Very well, sir, I shall obey your orders. [He goes towards the door.]

Count: Germon, you saw her as she went off?

Germon: I did, sir.

Count: Did she seem dejected? did she weep?

Germon: She behaved still better, sir; a few tears dropped from her, but she strove as much as she could to repress them.

Count: Did she let fall anything that betrayed her sentiments? did you remark—

Germon: What, sir?

Count: Did she say anything of me?

Germon: Yes, sir; a great deal.

Count: Tell me, then, rascal, what did she say?

Germon: That you were her master, her best and kindest benefactor; that she shall forget everything—but your cruelty.

Count: Away—be sure you take care she never returns; [Germon going out] and hark'ee, Germon.

Germon: Sir.

Count: One word more: remember, if, by chance, as you are conducting her, one Philip Hombert should follow you, that you treat him in a proper manner.

Germon: O, sir, I'll use him most politely, and treat him with a good drubbing, that you may depend on: I'll do the business honestly, I warrant you: young Hombert, you say?

Count: The same.

Germon: Very well: I have not the honor to know him, but the first man I see will I trim most heartily, and afterwards make him tell me his name. [He goes towards the door and comes back.] This young Hombert, I'll lay my life, is some lover of hers, a beau, a prig, I suppose, the cock of the village. Let me alone to deal with him.

Count: Do as I bid you, and immediately.

Germon: I thought there was some lover in the case—and Blaise, too, puts in his claim, I suppose. Ay: they always love their equals better than their masters.

Count: Begone, I tell you.

SCENE III.

The Count: [Alone.] He's in the right, and has hit on the true cause of my unhappiness, but I shall myself be the punisher of my own folly. I must now marry the baroness; it is determined, and I can't avoid it: 'tis dreadful; but I have deserved it; 'twill at least be a convenient match: she's not very tractable indeed, but every man may rule, if he has a mind to it; and he who has resolution may, at any time, be master in his own house.

SCENE IV.

The Count, Baroness, Marchioness.

Marchioness: Well, son, you are going to marry this lady here?

Count: Yes, madam.

Marchioness: This night she is to be your wife and my daughter-in-law?

Baroness: If you approve of it, madam; I suppose I shall have your consent.

Marchioness: Why, I must give it, I think: but to-morrow I shall take my leave of you.

Count: Your leave, madam, why so?

Marchioness: I shall take my Nanine with me: since you have thought fit to turn her out of doors, I shall take her under my protection: I have a match in my eye for her: I propose marrying her to the young chief justice, nephew to the attorney-general, Jean Roc Souci; he whose father met with that comical adventure at Corbeil; you must have heard of him: yes, I will take care of this poor child, I'm determined: she is a jewel, and deserves to be well set. I'll marry her off immediately. Your servant.

Count: My dear mother, don't be in a passion: leave me to manage my own affairs, and let Nanine go into a convent.

Baroness: Indeed, madam, you may believe us, such a girl as Nanine is not fit to go into a family.

Marchioness: Ha! why, what's the matter?

Baroness: O a little affair only.

Marchioness: But pray–

Baroness: O nothing at all.

Marchioness: Nothing! a great deal, I'm afraid: I understand you mighty well: some little indiscretion I suppose: nothing more likely, for to be sure, she's very handsome. Ay, ay, we are all frail; we tempt, and are tempted; the heart has its weakness: young girls are always a little coquettish: but come, it is not so bad as you make it; tell me fairly, what my poor child has done?

Count: I tell you, madam?

Marchioness: You seem, after all, at the bottom to have some regard for the girl, and perhaps you may–

SCENE V.

The Count, Marchioness, Baroness, Marin. [Booted.]

Marin: I've done it, sir; it's all agreed for.

Marchioness: What's agreed for?

Baroness: Ay, what, sir, what?

Marin: Why, sir, I've done as you ordered me, spoke to the tradesmen, and you'll have your equipage tomorrow.

Baroness: What equipage?

Marin: Everything, madam, that your future spouse had ordered; six fine horses, and a charming berlin; I'm sure your ladyship will like it; it's very fine; the panels all varnished by Martin: the diamonds, too, are brilliant, and well-chosen; and the new stuffs quite in taste.–O nothing comes up to them.

Baroness: [To the count.] And had you ordered all this?

Count: I had–[Aside] but for whom!

Marin: Everything will come to-morrow morning in the coach, and will be ready for your wedding in the evening: O there's nothing like Paris for getting everything at a minute's warning, if you have but money. As I came back, I called on the lawyer; he's just by, finishing your affair.

Baroness: It has hung a long time in suspense.

Marchioness: [Aside.] I wish it would hang these forty years.

Marin: In the hall I met a poor old man, sighing and in tears; he has waited a long time, he says, and begs to speak to you.

Baroness: An impertinent fellow! let him go about his business: he has chosen the wrong time to trouble us now.

Marchioness: Why, so, madam? have a little consideration: son, let me tell you, it's very wrong to repulse poor people in this manner; I have told you over and over, when you were a child, you ought to treat them with indulgence; hear what they have to say; be courteous, and affable to them: are not they men as well as yourself? we don't know perhaps whom we affront, and may repent our hardness of heart: the proud never prosper. [To Marin.] Go, see to that old man.

Marin: I will, ma'am. [He goes out.]

Count: Forgive me, madam, my respects are always due to you, and I am ready to see this man, in spite of my present embarrassment.

SCENE VI.

The Count, Marchioness, Baroness, A Peasant.

Marchioness: [To the Peasant.] Come, come, speak, don't be afraid.
Peasant: O my lord, for heaven's sake, hear me; permit me to fall at your feet, and to give you back—

Count: Rise, friend; I'll not be knelt to; do not imagine me capable of such pride: you seem to be an honest man, do you want employment in my family? who are you?

Marchioness: Cheer up, man.

Peasant: Alas! sir, I am the father of—Nanine.

Count: You?

Baroness: Your daughter's a slut.

Peasant: This, sir, is what I feared: this is the cruel stroke that has wounded my poor heart: I thought indeed so much money could not fairly belong to one in her condition: we little folks soon lose our integrity when we come among the great.

Baroness: There he's right enough: but still he's a deceiver, for Nanine is not his daughter, she was an orphan.

Peasant: It is too true, she was so: I left her with her poor relatives in her infant years, having lost her mother, with all my fortune; obliged by necessity, I went to serve abroad; and as I would not have her pass for the daughter of a soldier, forbade her ever to mention my name.

Marchioness: Why so? for my part, I respect a soldier: we stand in need of them sometimes.

Count: What is there shameful in the profession?

Peasant: It meets indeed with less honor than it deserves.

Count: The prejudice against them is inexcusable. I own, I esteem an honest soldier, who hazards his life in the defence of his king and country, much more than an important, self-sufficient scoundrel, whose knavish industry sucks up the blood of his fellow subjects.

Marchioness: You must have been in a great many battles: let me have an account of them all; I long to hear it.

Peasant: In my present unhappy condition you must excuse me: let it suffice to inform you, that I received a thousand promises of advancement; but, without friends, how was it possible to rise? thrown amongst the common crowd, all I could do was to distinguish myself, and honor my only reward.

Marchioness: You were then well-born?

Baroness: Fie: how can you think so! well-born indeed!

Peasant: No, madam: but I was born of honest parents, and merited—a better daughter.

Marchioness: Could you have had a better?

Count: Well! go on.

Marchioness: A better than Nanine?

Count: Prithee, go on.

Peasant: My daughter, I understood, was brought up here, and treated in the kindest manner; I thought myself happy, and blessed heaven for your goodness, and paternal care of her; I came to the neighboring village, full of hopes and fears; I own I trembled for her dangerous youth; and, by this lady's intimation, find I had but too much reason; it has shocked me to the soul; but I thought a hundred louis d'ors, besides diamonds, was a treasure too great to be fairly come by: she could never be mistress of them, but at the expense of her innocence: the bare suspicion makes me shudder; if it be so, I shall die with grief and shame: but I came as soon as possible, to give them you back again: they are yours, therefore, I beseech you, take them: if my daughter is to blame, punish me, but don't ruin her.

Marchioness: O my dear son, I cannot bear this; it overpowers me.

Baroness: What is all this? a dream? a trick?

Count: O what have I done?

Peasant: [Taking out the purse and the letter.] Here, sir, take them.

Count: I take them! no: they were given to her, and she has made a noble use of them: was it to you, then, the message was delivered? who brought it?

Peasant: Your gardener, sir, in whom Nanine ventured to confide.

Count: Was it directed to you?

Peasant: It was, I own it, sir.

Count: O grief! O tenderness! what excess of virtue in them both! but now your name?—O I am lost, distracted.

Marchioness: Ay, your name. What mystery is this?

Peasant: Philip Hombert de Gatine.

Count: O my father!

Baroness: What does he say?

Count: How day breaks in upon me! I have done wrong, and I must make amends for it: O if you knew how culpable I have been! I have injured the sublimest virtue. [He steps aside, and speaks to one of his servants.] away: fly.

Baroness: What is all this emotion for?

Count: My coach immediately.

Marchioness: Now, madam, you must be her protectress: when we have done such an injury, we should blush at nothing so much as an imperfect repentance; my son often has his whims, which people are too apt to mistake for unpardonable follies; but at bottom he has a generous soul, and is naturally good; I can do what I please with him: you, my daughter-in-law, are not so well-disposed.

Baroness: I shall grow out of all patience: how confused and thoughtful he looks! what strange scheme now is he meditating upon? well, sir, what do you intend to do?

Marchioness: Ay, for Nanine?

Baroness: Make her a handsome present, and satisfy her.

Marchioness: That will be the least we can do.

Baroness: But as to seeing her that I never will: she shall not come nigh the castle: do you hear me?

Count: Yes, I hear you.

Marchioness: [Aside.] What a heart of stone!

Baroness: Don't give my suspicions cause to break out, sir. Ha! you hesitate.

Count: [After a pause of some time.] No, madam, I am resolved.

Baroness: That respect at least is owing to me; nay, to both of us.

Marchioness: And can you be so cruel, son?

Baroness: What step do you propose to take?

Count: 'Tis taken already: you know my heart, madam, and the frankness of it: I must be plain with you: I had promised you my hand; but the design of our marriage was only to put an end to a tedious lawsuit between us, which I will now do immediately, by willingly resigning to you all those rights and pretensions which were the foundation of it: even the interest shall be yours; I give up everything, take, and enjoy it: if we cannot be man and wife, let us at least live as friends and relatives: let everything that gave mutual uneasiness be forgotten; there is no reason why, because we can't love, we should hate each other.

Baroness: Your falsehood is what I expected: but I renounce your presents, and yourself: yes, traitor, I see now who you mean to live with, and how low your passion sinks you: go, and be a slave to her, I leave you to your unworthy choice. [She goes out.]

SCENE VII.

The Count, Marchioness, Philip Hombert.

Count: No, madam, 'tis not unworthy, my soul is not blinded by an idle passion: that virtue which it is my duty to reward ought to melt, but cannot debase me: what they call meanness in this old man constitutes his merit, and makes him truly noble: if I would be so, I must pay the price of it: where souls are thus ennobled by themselves, and distinguished by superior characters, we should pass over common rules: their birth, low as it is, when attended with such virtues, will make my family but more illustrious.

Marchioness: What are you talking about?

SCENE VIII.

the count, marchioness, nanine, philip hombert.

Count: [To his mother.] Look at her, and guess.

Marchioness: [To Nanine.] My dearest child, come to my arms: but she is strangely clothed, and yet how handsome she looks, and modest too!

Nanine: [Pays her respects to the Marchioness, and then runs to her father.] O nature demands my first acknowledgments, my dear father!

Philip Hombert: O heaven! my daughter! O sir, you have made me amends for forty years' afflictions.

Count: Ay, but how must I repair the injury I have done to such exalted virtue! to come back in this dress, how mean it is, but she adorns it; Nanine does honor to everything: speak, my Nanine, can your goodness pardon the affront?

Nanine: Can you, sir, doubt my forgiveness of it? I never thought, after all your bounty to me, you could injure me.

Count: If you have indeed forgotten the wrong I did you, give me a proof of it: once more, and only once, I take upon me to command you; but this once you must swear—to obey me.

Philip Hombert: I am sure she owes it to you, and her gratitude—

Nanine: [To her father.] He need not doubt, sir, of my obedience.

Count: I shall depend on it: let me tell you then, that all your duty is not yet paid: I have seen you on your knees to my mother, and to your own father; one thing still remains for you, and that is, now, before them, to embrace—your husband.

Nanine: Who? I?

Marchioness: Are you in earnest? can it be?
Philip Hombert: O my child!

Count: [To his mother.] By your permission, madam.

Marchioness: My dear child, the family will be in a strange uproar about it.

Count: O when they see Nanine, they must approve.

Philip Hombert: What a stroke of fortune! O sir, I never thought you could descend thus low.

Count: You promised to obey, and I must have it so.

Marchioness: My son.

Count: My happiness, madam, depends on this important moment: interest alone, we know, has made a thousand marriages; we have seen the wisest men consult fortune and character only: her character is irreproachable; and as to fortune, she wants it not: justice and inclination shall do what avarice has so often done before: let me, then, madam, have your consent, and finish all.

Nanine: No, madam, you must not consent; indeed you must not; oppose his passion, oppose mine: let me entreat you, do: love has blinded him, do you, madam, remove the veil: let me live far from him, and at a distance only adore his virtues: you know my condition; you see my father: can I, ought I, ever to wish to call you mother?

Marchioness: Yes; you can, you ought: it is enough: I can hold out no longer: this last generosity has entirely subdued me: it tells me how much I ought to love: it is as singular, as extraordinary, as Nanine herself.

Nanine: Then, madam, I obey; my heart can no longer resist the power of love.

Marchioness: Let this happy day be the worthy recompense of virtue, but let it not be made a precedent.

End

www.ingramcontent.com/pod-product-compliance
Lightning Source LLC
Chambersburg PA
CBHW031436040426
42444CB00006B/833